5 Simple Steps to Find a Top-Performing Stock: How to Identify Investments that Can Double Quickly for Personal Success

Brian Nichols

I0462380

Table of Contents

Chapter 1 – Not Your Typical Investing Book

Any investment book you read is almost certain to discuss balance sheets, cash flow, valuation metrics, etc., and within the pages, the reader is given some sort of formula or strategy that is based on the information and the investment paradigm used in the book. This particular formula then, can be based on value, contrarian, or some other type of investing strategy. So, in a nutshell, most investment books are presented the same way, albeit a unique twist.

In fact, I should know, back in 2012 I wrote "*Taking Charge With Value Investing: How to Choose the Best Investments According to Price, Performance, & Valuation to Build a Winning Portfolio*" for McGraw-Hill – published in 2013. Aside from a few unique tools and a psychological twist, it pretty much followed the same guidelines that are used by all financial authors.

With that said I was immensely pleased with my work; feeling as though it had served the purpose in which it was written. Yet, as I discussed many of my top stock picks, those that have become very public, while choosing to disclose my contact information and websites, the feedback I received from readers was a bit shocking to me.

Readers were particularly interested in knowing (how) I chose my Value of the Year stocks more than anything else. They were not so much as interested in the definition of cash flow, or 200 other pages of detail. Instead, they wanted a straight forward answer to their question.

When I first started to receive these messages, I thought I made a mistake with how the book was written, not addressing the most basic of questions for beginners;

making the material too complex. So, I took a step back and realized that what the reader really wanted was a step-by-step HOW TO CHOOSE such investments; not the same ole investment book; only worded differently and with a different cover that they had been reading for decades.

This HOW TO CHOOSE the very best once-in-a-year investment question is what led me to this point, trying to figure out the best method for explaining how I knew to buy certain stocks when I did, and the degree of value that was present. Initially, I thought another 50,000 plus worded book with a big-name publisher would be necessary, but then I realized that people don't have a week to read and study such material; the people want answers quick, easy and immediately!

Furthermore, I realized that my process for finding each top stock performer is simple, and that it can be summed up in less than 10,000 words, or one-fifth that of a typical investing book. As a result, you won't find any page-wasting content in this book, but rather a straight forward answer that helps you with your future investing endeavors.

This book will use my personal experiences, not hypothetical situations, to explain how and why I made certain decisions, with investments that have been the most lucrative. With that said, you might think there's a long list to obtaining such success. In fact, there are only FIVE steps, the simple steps I have followed with each and every one of my six top Value of the Year selections; all of which have significantly outperformed the market in their respective years; an average of more than 150%.

In 2012, Sprint Corporation (NASDAQ: S) was chosen as my top annual selection, which was long before its enormous run higher and the takeover by Softbank. In fact, Sprint traded at just $2.30 when I jumped on the bandwagon, but by the end of the year with it appreciating more than 150%, there were far more people propitious toward Sprint.

In 2013, I chose two stocks: Alcatel-Lucent (NASDAQ: ALU) and Rite Aid (NYSE: RAD), which were two companies that just as many people thought were headed for bankruptcy as a turnaround. Yet, with stock gains of 300% and 400%, respectively, for Alcatel-Lucent and Rite Aid, those betting on a bankruptcy were sorely mistaken. Instead, those people betting against these companies could have made a lot of money had they followed four simple steps.

Finally, in 2014 it was a trio of stocks that made my highest of lists, none of which had the same 12-month multi-bagger upside as Alcatel-Lucent or Rite Aid, but presented incredible value after one of the best bull markets in history nonetheless. Already, Apple (NASDAQ: AAPL) and Restoration Hardware (NYSE: RH) have soared 30% each, and XPO Logistics (NYSE: XPO) has added another 25%. In fact, XPO Logistics was named my Value of the Decade back in 2011 with a price target of $100 long-term, and has since; more than tripled!

Therefore, you may be curious as to what exact steps did I used to find these top-market performers? Well, you're about to find out!

Chapter 2 – Step One

One of the great things about the stock market is that it's full of TV-like plots, or things you don't necessarily expect. You can find drama, such as the Carl Icahn and Bill Ackman Herbalife ordeal. If you tire of drama, you can find suspense with the announcement of key economic data, or the notes and speeches from the Federal Reserve. Or maybe you want action, like with the big time proxy fights that we see so often among activist investors.

For some, this is a nightmare, causing volatility and wild stock price swings that create fear in the minds of investors. But for others, it is a blessing in disguise, as it creates value, or better yet, it gives you the opportunity to identify value.

With that said, Step 1 in finding top market performers lies in the ability to embrace such chaos, identify the stocks that see big movement from key catalysts; those that are fundamental game changers for a specific company. I call this the "Unaccounted for Catalyst" and the market's willingness to catch-up when it was wrong. In other words, it is the process of identifying a crucial catalyst, and very likely; company-changing.

Sprint is a great history lesson

To explain, let's look at Sprint or a history lesson in simple terms. To put it lightly, Sprint was pathetic in 2011, as well as the years prior. The company had nothing: It was losing subscribers on a quarter-to-quarter basis, it was far from profitable, and its debt as a percentage of total assets continued to rise year-after-year-after-year. This rising debt left the company with few options, much like a person who is drowning in debt, unable to make the infrastructure or operational investments to catch its thriving peers like AT&T and Verizon.

Now, investors attributed Sprint's downfall to a number of different factors, whether it be management, its network, bad reputation, etc. But, anyone who had followed the telecom market in the years of 2011 and before, knew that the hottest best-selling must-have product was the iPhone and that those who had it thrived while those without it suffered.

In fact, Apple sold 72.3 million units in its fiscal year of 2011, ending in September, representing year-over-year growth of 81%, and in the year prior, 2010, it had seen growth of 93% year-over-year (Apple.com, n.d.). Therefore, the fact that prior to late-2011 Sprint did not have rights to sell the iPhone meant that it was at a significant disadvantage to its two larger competitors. Sprint simply did not benefit from the iPhone's unprecedented growth, or the high demand and excitement that surrounded it. Not to mention, retailers, such as RadioShack, were starting to blame Sprint for poor performance yet another sign that the days ahead were dark for the country's third largest service provider.

The bottom line is if Sprint wasn't going to sell the most sought after device, customers went elsewhere, as did future potential customers. Yet, despite its dwindling fundamentals and lacking rights to the iPhone, let me repeat that Sprint traded over $5 a share for much of early 2011, a price point that is crucial in explaining the opportunity that followed.

The game changer

With all of the doom and gloom surrounding Sprint, and since readers already know the outcome, you might be wondering what I saw as a great upside value during this time of hardship.

Honestly, the answer to that question is nothing! There was nothing from a fundamental or operational stance that I liked about Sprint: All of the problems I noted were still relevant. But, one thing changed: The Company gained rights to the iPhone, which thereby made it interesting, in giving it a fighting chance to retain subscribers and attract new ones.

This fact represents the first step in finding such game-changing value, and that is the unaccounted or unexpected catalyst, and as for Sprint, the iPhone was a big one!

Furthermore, by late-2011, the company's stock had fallen south of $2.50 due to the fundamental problems that are noted; people were essentially expecting a bankruptcy, counting down the days until its cash ran out. However, combined with the iPhone, Sprint had two key components that made it beyond interesting: (1) Sprint offered unlimited data at a fixed price, which competitors did not offer at the time, and (2) its stock had fallen from over $5 to below $2.50. Hence, if Sprint was worth $5 without the iPhone, my logic was that it would be worth an exceedingly lot more with the fastest growing and best-selling device in America.

The rest is history.

With all things considered, Sprint's turnaround in 2012 was not immediate. In fact, Sprint traded in a $2.30 to $3 range for the first six months of 2012. However, slowly but surely, the company began to see subscriber and revenue growth.

Specifically, in the second quarter of 2012 the stock soared doubled digits, kind of a breakout earnings report, as its postpaid net additions (subscribers) increased 68% over the quarter before it to 442,000. It was at this point that investors realized the advantage that Sprint gained with the iPhone, combined with unlimited data. But, had investors paid attention, connecting the obvious dots, and been patient their investment outcome would have been much more rewarding.

Therefore, Wall Street was pleased and the stock soared higher, even into 2013, surpassing $11.00 at its height. The key takeaway from Sprint is that catalysts come every day, and when the market doesn't expect it, or undervalues its implications, a stock can see unprecedented stock gains in both short-term and long-term.

These are the things you want to watch out for, and should be the first step in your research. Notably, these catalysts don't always move a stock initially, but if a stock is beaten down, unnoticed, or undervalued and one of these company-changing events occur, it's imperative to be there for the reaping.

One for the road

With that said, I want to be certain that you understand how to identify these unaccounted for catalysts, including its cause and effect. Therefore, let's look at one more quick Apple-related example, involving GT Advanced (NASDAQ: GTAT) and Corning Incorporated (NYSE: GLW).

One of the most crucial components of the iPhone, and all smartphones, is the glass that protects the device. In recent years, Corning's Gorilla Glass has been used on not only iPhones but also other popular models like the Samsung Galaxy. Gorilla Glass is known for being strong, durable, and scratch resistant. However, sapphire is even thinner, stronger, and even more scratch resistant.

Up until now, manufacturers haven't used sapphire except for home buttons and the camera lens due to high expenses. In 2013, Apple signed a deal with GT Advanced to use its furnaces to produce sapphire; fueling the belief that sapphire would be used on either the iPhone 6 or future models. While GT Advanced received $578 million (Apple to build new manufacturing facility in Arizona with solar-power, will create 2000+ jobs, 2013) up-front for the deal and saw its stock soar, behind the news, investors practicing Step 1 in finding deep value, could have realized the extensive fundamental upside that lied within this deal.

Specifically, GT Advanced earned just 11% of its revenue prior to the Apple deal from sapphire, or $28.9 million, but after the deal, with Apple guided for revenue of $700 million, with 80% coming from sapphire (9to5mac.com, 2013). In other words, GT Advanced's revenue from sapphire increased from $28.9 million to more than $550 million. Hence, the Apple deal was unexpected, as was the immense fundamental gains that followed, meaning this was a game changer for GT Advanced. Furthermore, long-term investors could have considered the implications that could possibly follow the deal, such as other manufacturers switching to sapphire to remain competitive with Apple;

the end result would have been another 100% stock gains over the following year in shares of GT Advanced.

With that said, I cannot stress enough the importance of keeping your eyes and ears open for catalysts that may have a profound positive or negative effect on companies. If a stock is beaten to a pulp, and the company announces a breakthrough partnership, then buy it!

Always think of how a catalyst could affect an underlying business, and if that catalyst is meaningful in significantly improving the business as a whole as well as long-term. The iPhone news for Sprint and the partnerships with GT Advanced were obvious, but perhaps missed by many investors. Therefore, an easy way to identify many of these catalysts is to watch for large intraday stock pops, find out why the stock popped, ask yourself what that news means for the company, and if obviously meaningful, you can then go on to step 2.

Chapter 3 -- Step Two

If Step 1 is to simply identify game-changing catalysts, and to determine whether it can have a profound effect on an underlying business, then Step 2 has to be predicting the amount of upside that can be created.

This Step has great significance because it really ties the importance of being a value investor into finding top stock performers; the company must be fundamentally cheap!

In Step 1 we touched on this by noting that Sprint's stock had fallen from $5 to $2.50 when it gained the iPhone. However, price does not necessarily indicate value. A stock can easily soar 100% and still be cheap. Conversely, a stock can fall 50% and still be too expensive. To explain Step 2 – identify clear and obvious value -- there is perhaps no better example than Rite Aid.

Rite Aid turns it around

In the five years prior to 2012, Rite Aid lost nearly 80% of its valuation, and like Sprint, Rite Aid was a company that many thought was destined for bankruptcy. During that five year period, Rite Aid never posted a quarterly profit, and was plagued with lower customer traffic, inefficient prescription processing, and poor front-end retail sales. So, as quarterly losses continued to exist, the business as a whole also suffered.

Then, the company's third quarter of 2012 was announced, which included net income of $61.9 million on revenue of $6.2 billion (riteaid.com, n.d.). While $61.9 million is a large profit for most companies, the sheer size of Rite Aid meant that its profit margin was less than 1% during this particular quarter. Notably, the company's revenue did fall 1.2%, but I myself, was more concerned with what drove the company's $61.9 million profit from a $52 million loss in the year prior; especially after so many quarters of net losses.

As I dug deeper, listened to the conference call and read the SEC filings, I realized that the quarter wasn't a fluke, and that the company had been improving over the last few quarters. Moreover, this improvement was a result of the patent cliff, a period between 2011 and 2016 where $133 billion of branded drug sales either lost or will lose patent protection (Stone, n.d.).

Importantly, generic drugs carry much higher margins than brand drugs. Generics are bought in bulk, lowering the price of logistics, and have greater flexibility for mark-up pricing. Therefore, this was a big deal, and profitability, served as an unexpected catalyst (Step 1) that could take a beaten down Rite Aid stock much higher.

But how high can it go?

While many investors were satisfied and took profits with Rite Aid's intraday gains of 16% following its third quarter of 2012, I saw the quarter as an opportunity to invest in a business that was obviously improving, yet was not priced in any way as a profitable one. Therefore, I was happy to buy the shares that others were selling at $1.20

Perhaps the only problem was that I could not analyze it on a price/earnings basis due to it being incomparable to its competitors. After all, it's not fair to compare and contrast Rite Aid's margins against the industry's elite after just one decent quarter. As a result, I turned to sales for my valuation analysis, which I believe is the most crucial metric for investors who are analyzing value and a company's upside potential.

Specifically, the market valued each $1 of revenue for Rite Aid at $0.05, or price/sales of 0.05. Meanwhile, Walgreen Co. (NYSE: WAG), who is considered to be an extremely efficient company, was valued at $0.40 for every $1, or eight times the premium of Rite Aid.

Consequently, if Rite Aid was headed to bankruptcy, then it was valued appropriately, but if in fact it had found consistent profits, then it was considerably undervalued. At the time, I considered a higher mix of generic drugs; thus, giving reason to believe that higher margins and profits were more than likely for Rite Aid.

Therefore, determining "what is fair value" becomes the question. The answer to that question varies and is dependent upon multiple factors such as margins, revenue growth, cash-flow, etc., as it relates to its competitors. However, even without growth and near breakeven margins, Rite Aid was worth far more than one-eighth of its rivals.

In fact, even a one-third discount would have given Rite Aid an attractive valuation, but that would have also meant that Rite Aid's stock would have to increase at least 125% while Walgreen traded flat with zero sales growth, which was not the case. Hence, if my analysis tells me that Rite Aid would be a good buy following a 125% gain, then clearly it is a great opportunity prior to those large gains being created. In other words, I identified great upside value in Rite Aid based on valuation, which just so happens to be Step 2.

No one expected this

Today, shares of Rite Aid trade near $7. The company has seen revenue growth in each of its last three quarters, including pharmacy sales rising in excess of 3% in each month of 2014 (so far). Moreover, Rite Aid's operating margin of 2.76% represents an increase of more than 300 basis points from 2012, which is incredible; given the historically low margin business of pharmacies.

You see, Rite Aid's return to profitability had a domino effect. Due to its profits the company was able to invest in infrastructure, new technology for its employees, and upgrade its stores, driving traffic higher, which thereby created growth.

However, it all started with one positive quarter of profits and a stock that was clearly way too cheap, relatively to its competitors. With that said, a company can always use aggressive accounting to manipulate profits, so although a P/E ratio is important and a Wall Street favorite, revenues never lie. For Rite Aid, its high revenues relative to valuation showed us that with a little bit of improvement the stock could soar a long way. Once those improvements occur, the cheapness of the stock becomes apparent, as a little bit of profits relative to revenue translate to a lot relative to the valuation.

Growth vs value

Nonetheless, comparing valuations to revenue is a good tool, and if a company is growing fast you can also take that into consideration in your analysis. To explain, I want to provide a relatively simple valuation model as a rule of thumb based on revenue and growth looking at Dollar Tree (NYSE: DLTR) and Walmart (nyse: WMT).

First off, you can learn how fast a company is expected to grow revenue in Yahoo! Finance. Simply search for a company, and then on the left hand side click "Analyst Estimates". It will tell you the expected growth rates for the upcoming quarter, the full-year, and the following year. For investors, it's the full year and following year that gets our utmost attention.

With that said, Dollar Tree is expected to grow revenue 8.5% this year. Meanwhile, Walmart is expected to grow 2.2% in the same period. If we look further ahead to 2015, Dollar Tree's expected growth of 8.7% is expected to more than double that of Walmart; this follows a four-fold growth premium this year.

Albeit, to say that Dollar Tree is "worth" three times the sales multiple of Walmart wouldn't be unrealistic. Currently, Walmart trades at 0.50 times sales while Dollar Tree trades at 1.4 times sales. Therefore, Dollar Tree presents slightly more upside value that Walmart based on this model, although not much.

However, if a game-changing catalyst, let's say the acquisition of Family Dollar, comes around, the outlook may change, as Dollar Tree's revenue and profits would essentially double or more. This is a key example of how a company may trade at "fair value" one day, but how a key game-changing catalyst can change the landscape.

Now, in regards to Rite Aid at 0.05 times sales, Walgreen was growing about four times faster, meaning it was worth 0.20 times sales relative to Rite Aid, although it traded at 0.40. Clearly, this formula proved accurate in this case, as Rite Aid quickly soared with large gains until reaching a current valuation that is likely fair, relative to its competitors.

With that said, you can use this growth equals valuation premium logic with any metric of importance, such as P/E ratios, return on equity, or operating cash flow.

The important question is how much of a premium should be rewarded for performance? And even if the performance gap is wide, how wide should the valuation gap be? Sometimes it's obvious, like Rite Aid, and other times it is not, like Dollar Tree. However, if it's not obvious, and the gap is not wide, then chances are we are not talking about a stock with unprecedented 12-month upside, unless Dollar Tree acquires Family Dollar.

If obvious, continue to Step 3.

Chapter 4 -- Step Three

One thing you may have noticed during the thorough conversations of Rite Aid and Sprint is that both companies had a fundamental edge that was given to them outside of their respective catalysts.

For example, Sprint gained the iPhone, which was a direct advantage to the company due to its lacking of the product. However, this was only relevant because the market's overall demand for the iPhone was excessive, which was a macro-related strength that fell into the company's lap.

In regards to Rite Aid, profit was the catalyst. However, it was also the beneficiary of the patent cliff, an event that it did nothing to earn. The effect of the patent cliff was profits, but the cliff itself was a macro-related event that helped to compliment the profits that followed.

Therefore, as we look ahead to Step 3 -- identifying a market or macro advantage, and examining the strong macro-related trends -- keep in mind that a company might have a catalyst, but the key is knowing whether that catalyst is sustainable; possibly generating long-term, once-in-a-year type of gains, is pondering whether or not the overall market will give it a natural push of sorts.

To thoroughly explain this Step and its importance, let's look at Restoration Hardware, and maybe add a little Michael Kors to this mix.

The demand of luxury plus home improvement

During the bull market of the last few years there has been much strength; industries within the automotive and aerospace sectors have thrived, as well as with non-cyclical sectors, like pharmaceuticals. For the most part retail has been wretched, as the rise of e-commerce has pretty much obviated any and all growth, due to the price war it created that offset improved traffic.

However, trendy areas in retail like luxury and categories such as home improvement have been areas of retail with consistent strength. In the first six months of 2014, the U.S. retail report showed 3.8% growth in the building material, garden equipment, and supply dealers business (U.S. Census Bureau News, 2014). For investors, this strength is a good sign to look deep within the sector to find value or upside investment opportunities.

For example, a lot of investors like Home Depot (NYSE: HD), a company whose guidance for 4.6% comparable growth in 2014 exceeds the overall market (Home Depot, 2013). The problem with Home Depot as an investment is that it's not especially cheap, nor does it have explosive growth for a stock trading at 21 times earnings.

With that said, I liked the home improvement space as a place for opportunity, which led me to Restoration Hardware, a company that combined home improvement with another one of retail's strengths: Luxury!

Unlike Sprint and Rite Aid, Restoration Hardware is an explosive growth company, maybe the fastest growing company of its size within the entire retail sector. As a reference, the company has grown comparable-store sales by 57% over the last two years, and what's remarkable is that it has done so without the addition of one single new store; which currently is comprised of 69 stores.

Like Michael Kors in the handbag space, Restoration Hardware's approach of working with unique suppliers means that its styles are not replicated, and the company has become the go-to home improvement retailer for the wealthy. Therefore, we are combining two strengths of the economy, meaning Restoration Hardware has a strong macro-related advantage in its favor to meet Step 3 of the requirements in finding a top stock.

What about Steps 1 & 2?

As we progress through these Steps, it is imperative for me to point out the significance in that each and every one of these companies possessed all the Steps needed in order to qualify as a top stock, which ultimately drove large gains.

Albeit, I was actually bullish on Restoration Hardware following its IPO in 2012, as I already knew it had a growing presence with luxury consumers and in the home improvement space that was also thriving. Since then the stock has soared 170%, and during this process, the most impressive facet of its business is that it's managed to grow aggressively without adding any new stores, meaning it continuously drives more consumers into existing stores, produces larger order sizes, and sees increased direct-to-consumer sales.

But, what made it so attractive in 2014 is that Step 1 & 2 also became relevant in the investment discussion, which was lacking when I made my original investment in 2013. Back in 2013, the stock nearly doubled, but it was mainly from growth, and driven by macro-related factors.

However, the key that really fits and puts the Restoration Hardware investment puzzle together was expansion, and is why the stock will not only soar in 2014, but also in 2015 and beyond. Restoration Hardware's management had already begun to mention on conference calls and presentations that it was looking to expand, and then gave specific details at the end of their 2013 fiscal year (Seeking Alpha, 2014).

Specifically, CEO Gary Friedman said, *"This year, we will open new Galleries in Greenwich [Conn.], Los Angeles, and our first next generation Full Line Design Gallery in Atlanta. Additionally, we are significantly expanding the size our New York Gallery, adding two additional floors to our top performing store in the [c]ompany. We now have signed leases for five next generation Full Line Design Galleries and are in negotiations for an additional 25 locations."*

So, if Restoration Hardware can grow 57% over a two-year period and generate revenue of $1.5 billion with 69 stores, what then, can be accomplished after expanding with another 25 locations; while also making existing stores larger? Another element to this question surrounds the fact that Restoration Hardware had in no way found its peak revenue per existing store, as it continues to grow at 20% plus at their current existing stores. This means the $21 million they earn per store on average, is most certain to rise in the years ahead.

In the company's long-term guidance its CEO gave us a little hint as to how much larger the company could grow by combining same-store sales growth and expansion. He said that under the current expansion plan, Restoration Hardware will earn up to $5 billion in revenue with an operating margin in the mid-teens. So, with 69 current stores, and the plan to add another 30 during this initial expansion plan, Restoration Hardware's revenue per store, on average, will more than double to $50 million, meaning explosive growth for many years to come. Who knows, the company might expand another 30 stores or possibly even decide to expand globally, driving immensely even more growth.

Therefore, valued at $2.2 billion, Restoration Hardware was trading at 0.4 times peak sales – relative to its initial expansion plan and about three times peak earnings. Clearly, this is comparatively very cheap in relation to Home Depot, which is trading at 20 times earnings.

As a result, the valuation relative to its peak outlook and the catalyst of expansion served as Steps 2 and 1, respectively, for what must be found in order to identify a top tier once-in-a-year type of performer. In retrospect, Restoration Hardware has all the makings of a future big-time retailer; one that could perhaps, in the years ahead compete with the current top two home improvement retailers; Lowe's and Home Depot.

Chapter 5 -- Step Four

Hopefully, at this point you have a good idea at how Steps 1, 2, & 3 all fit together, and why they are imperative in finding a top stock performer. Now we are moving to the final step, the one that usually separates the pretenders from the contenders.

This final Step is all about direction, strategy, and management, but also the level of faith you have in management that they can actually deliver on the goals they set. Because after all, anyone can have a plan, and sell investors a pipedream, but having the knowledge, infrastructure, and willingness to execute is a completely different story. Hence, if all the pieces fit in place, it can be the difference between a solid stock performer in a company that has all first three Steps, and a once-in-a-year or lifetime type of investment.

To explain this philosophy, and its importance, let's look at XPO Logistics (NYSE: XPO), whose CEO Bradley Jacobs is perhaps the best possible example in identifying strong management with a winning plan.

A new face, new identity

Before XPO Logistics was created, it was Express-1 Expedited Solutions, and in 2011 had a market capitalization of under $100 million with annual revenue of $177 million. In that year, 2011, Bradley Jacobs invested $150 million of his own money into the company, and thereby became CEO and Chairman of the board (Jacobs to Become Chairman and Chief Executive Officer, 2011).

With that said, Jacobs did not come in with the ambitions of keeping everything the same, but rather an aggressive plan to grow the freight brokerage business to billions of revenue through acquisitions and cold starts. His goal was to become dominant in the $50 billion a year U.S. freight brokerage market and relevant in the $150 billion global market. Notably, if it would have been anyone except Jacobs with this plan, investors would have laughed him out of town.

Instead, with Jacobs being one of the most accomplished entrepreneurs in history; taking nothing and turning it into something, many such as me, jumped on the bandwagon at the very start.

Prior to XPO Logistics, Jacobs had built four other billion dollar companies with United Waste and United Rentals being the most notable. Jacobs started United Waste in 1989 with $20 million, but over the course of nearly a decade, he completed roughly 250 acquisitions and then sold it for more than $2 billion to Waste Management Inc. Then, with a $50 million start-up investment, he created the world's largest equipment rental company, United Rentals. Today, United Rentals is a publicly traded company with a market capitalization north of $10 billion.

Granted, what makes Jacobs's strategy so successful is not the 500 acquisitions he has completed in his career (McCracken, 2014), but rather the ability to identify and enter big fragmented markets that are growing faster than GDP, and then having the know how to grow those acquisitions larger once incorporated with the core business.

During his tenure at XPO Logistics, I have spoken with him on countless occasions, and he always tells me that buying revenue is not the goal. Instead, he buys companies with infrastructure that can be used, or services that add to XPO's original services, thus giving customers more options. As a result, by combining networks, Jacobs and his team are able to grow those acquisitions two to three times its novel size.

Perhaps the best example is one he gave me following XPO's acquisition of Pacer International (Nichols, 2014), who is an intermodal specialist. Pacer made $27 million in 2013, but Jacobs explained that in order to get more from Pacer its empty miles must improve. According to Jacobs, 39% of Pacer's miles are empty, meaning miles traveled that create no revenues, and this compares to an industry average of 25%.

He said that for every 100 basis points of improvement that Pacer gains an extra $1 million in profits. Therefore, by giving XPO's customers the option of intermodal and by making XPO's customer base larger with future acquisitions, those empty miles will improve. In essence, the acquisitions create diversity, provide customers with options, and ensure that customers have no reason to use more than one provider, that being XPO Logistics.

So within just three years under his leadership at XPO Logistics, the company has completed 13 acquisitions and now has a revenue-run rate of more than $3 billion! In fact, during its last quarter the company grew revenue by 324% year-over-year to $581 million (edgaronline.com, 2014). Clearly his plan is working, which is a plan you don't see often on Wall Street, but is what you want to see in a Value of the Decade type of stock.

So what about the other steps?

When I invested in XPO Logistics all four Steps in finding a great investment were inexplicably evident.

Step 1 – We had the catalyst of Jacobs's investment, including his long-term goals and a history of success.

Step 2 – XPO Logistics now has a long-term goal to reach revenue of more than $7 billion, so with a $1.6 billion market capitalization; it trades at only 0.22 times peak sales today. For a company's growth such as theirs, we usually see obscene price multiples, some north of 10 times sales, further showing XPO's level of value.

Step 3 – We also have the economic or macro advantage, as the freight brokerage market is fragmented with countless acquisition opportunities and is growing at twice the rate of the transportation sector.

Step 4 – We have Bradley Jacobs, of course, a leader with a powerful vision that will create market leading returns for many years to come.

Therefore, we have each four steps checked off our list with XPO Logistics, and an easy way to identify the very best possible upside.

Chapter 6 -- Putting It All Together

While this book is short, I hope you find it useful, packed with valuable information that can be used in your investment endeavors.

I would like to add that this formula can be used in any industry of the market except biotechnology. With biotechnology, investing is more about speculation, and the presence of value can be identified based on a biotechnology company's chances of an FDA approval and its valuation relative to peak sales potential for its lead drug candidate.

In theory, a company is at max value when trading at three times a lead drug candidate's peak sales potential, which is near equivalent to the premium of big pharma. Hence, if the drugs chances of an FDA approval are high, so long as the stock trades at less than one times the peak sales potential, you can most likely find considerable gains long-term.

With that said, I have shown you examples of each Step with Sprint, Rite Aid, Restoration Hardware, XPO Logistics, and Dollar Tree along with GT Advanced to some degree, all of which operate in different industries of the market. As for my Values of the Year, I already discussed everything with XPO Logistics, but here is a quick review of how the companies met each Step.

Sprint

- Gaining the iPhone as a device to sell

- Had lost 50% of valuation by the time it gained the iPhone

- Smartphone sales was a growth industry of market, with iPhone sales higher by more than 80%

- CEO strategy of offering unlimited data during a time when consumers were increasing their use of smartphones online. Sprint was first of the big three telecom companies to execute this strategy.

Alcatel-Lucent

- Alcatel-Lucent received $2 billion from Goldman Sachs to undergo a massive restructuring process.

- The company was incredibly cheap at just 0.20 times the sales in an industry trading at 1.5-2.0 times sales. Alcatel-Lucent had several segments weighing its business down, wherefore, ridding itself of those segments, the growth industries would became more visible, and make the company more valuable.

- Alcatel has become a leader in routers, growing more than 15% annually with high margins in mid-teens. Although it accounts for less than 20% of total revenue, a valuation analysis of one of its peers, Juniper, has reputable exposure and strength in routers, confirms that Alcatel's routing business alone was worth more than its entire company. The only wildcard surrounding Alcatel is whether that router business can stay strong.

- The new CEO's strategy to downsize Alcatel-Lucent was ingenious. Prior management had been hesitant to downsize at all, following the Alcatel and Lucent merger. However, the company was too big, and with several segments operating at a net loss, and others losing money year-after-year, it made more sense to sell those assets to companies who could use them, and then pay off debt to become a leaner and meaner company. The one thing that's yet to be seen is whether Alcatel will sell the right businesses, and if the divestments will occur quickly. Nonetheless, despite these minor concerns, the downsizing plan was smart. That, combined with its valuation provided significant upside potential in the year that followed.

Rite Aid

- The first quarter of profitability in 2012

- Trading at just 0.05 times the sales was unprecedented, valued for bankruptcy, gave the stock room for increase, as it plays catch-up to its peers Walgreen and CVS.

- The patent cliff meant higher margins

- Profitability meant that management had the money to restructure the business, such as putting iPads in the hands of employees, improving the merchandise, investing in infrastructure, etc. After one year of consistent profits in 2013 and large investments within this initiative, Rite Aid began to see year-over-year revenue growth to compliment higher margins, which took the stock even higher.

Restoration Hardware

- Expansion

- Traded at a ridiculously low multiple relative to peak sales potential

- Luxury + home improvement = success

- Management's strategy of using smaller and loyal vendors to create unique goods worked to its advantage. Also, Restoration Hardware is one of the only retailers that still actually use a catalog, and while this might fail with J.C. Penney, high-end consumers have gravitated to this model as a way to see the designs before buying. Overall, management's strategy is what allowed success.

Apple

- Launch of iPhone 6 and its expansion into China following a deal with China Mobile

- Apple's stock had been weighed down in 2013, leaving the technology giant trading at less than 10 times earnings minus cash. On just about every metric it was cheaper than other big tech companies like Microsoft and Google.

- Devices such as tablets and smartphones remains one of the strongest points of the market

- Tim Cook is no Steve Jobs, but he has smart people in high role positions and by building on the company's current ecosystem, with no plans to do anything too dramatic, the company should continue to thrive. Hence, Cook's plan to stay with what worked was likely his wisest executive decision.

As you should see, each company, although different, possessed each stock-moving catalyst I looked for in a top performer. An important factor is that investors can find good investments in companies that only have Steps 1 & 2 in their favor, and finding one that has all four is rare, which is why large gains are usually the such result.

Step 5!

Now, there is one more thing you must do, let's call it Step 5, and I'll go on to say that this is without question the most important discipline you can possibly practice, and that's finding a price target and having the guts to walk away from an investment, or knowing when to sell.

You see this is where psychology comes into play, and my former career as a counselor for the department of corrections becomes relevant, understanding why people make certain decisions, or so to say, the driving force.

Specifically, when a person finds and capitalizes on a top stock performer, or a multi-bagger, they almost develop a relationship with that company, a deep connection. I know it sounds strange, but investors, especially inexperienced retail investors looking to get rich in the stock market, develop a gamblers persona.

They can quickly forget all the bad investments or trades, and tend to focus on only the good. So when you find a top performer, it becomes almost like your bragging right, something that makes you feel good, you talk about it at the country club or at work, and find it nearly impossible to cut ties and move on to the next investment.

In my first book, "Taking Charge with Value Investing", I discuss psychology in great detail, and for nothing else it's a great read for understanding the key decisions you make which end up hurting your returns. For example, always set a target price that you will take profits, unless something drastic occurs to change the outlook for a particular company.

Next, instead of first thinking, "how high can this stock go", change your thought process to that of a short-seller, ask yourself, "how low can it go?" By doing this you reprogram yourself to minimize risk, looking at stock charts without the expectations for an uptrend, but rather preparing for a down-trending stock.

Perhaps my best examples are with Rite Aid and Alcatel-Lucent. In the case of Rite Aid, I knew that its downside was limited, and because of its enormous price/sales disconnect from Walgreen and others alike, I set a price target of $3 in 2012, which is well-documented, and took into consideration that even if profitable Rite Aid lacked growth and the same high margins of its competitors. Thus, at $3, its sales multiple was still considerably discounted from Walgreen.

Initially, I had set a sell order on Rite Aid at $3, but then the unexpected occurred: Rite Aid began to show consistent revenue growth, which was unseen at the time it first became profitable. This fact then changed the valuation landscape, because although it still wasn't worth the same premium as Walgreen or CVS, its growth made it far more valuable than 25% the premium of its competitors. As a result, I upped the target to $7, a 50% discount, and took profits at that point.

With Alcatel-Lucent, its price times sales multiple also trailed competitors like Cisco by a wide margin, much like Rite Aid to Walgreen. If in fact management followed through with its divestment plan then it seemed logical that Alcatel-Lucent's more profitable and faster growing businesses would outshine those that it sold to pay off debt, becoming more meaningful from a valuation perspective. However, a lot of questions remained as to which segments would be divested, therefore I gave it a $3.50 target, still much cheaper than its rivals.

Even with Sprint, I sold at $7, a set target. The stock clearly soared well beyond $7, but once the iPhone's year-over-year growth begun to decelerate rapidly, I knew that Sprint's existing fundamental woes would be visible.

The key takeaway is that even though all three stocks ended up trading beyond my selling point, I set the targets to have an exit plan, and to avoid becoming emotionally attached to either stock. As of today, Rite Aid trades below $7, Alcatel-Lucent at just $3.30, and Sprint at $5.70, meaning that once the hype died, my initial outlook was rather accurate.

In other words, don't get too caught up in what gains you might miss if a stock surpasses your target, just be happy with those you earned. Remember, the goal of investing is to make more money than you started with, so anytime you accomplish this feat, you win!

For the road

With that said, you are now ready to go out into the marketplace and find top values of your own. So when a company catches your eye with a big announcement, whether it causes a significant stock move or not, ask yourself how meaningful in long-term is that news? Then consider, is the company cheap relative to its peers? Does the company operate in an industry of strength or weakness, where it can ultimately build on the news that caught your attention? If all three questions appear favorable, try digging a little deeper, toward understanding management's plan, and how it'll work long-term.

Using this approach will take the difficulty out of investing. As investors, we have a tendency to make it more difficult than it has to be. Therefore, if you can fill your portfolio with stocks that meet each step, more than likely you'll not only outperform the market every year, but you'll find yourself making a substantial amount of money and living a far better life. Now that's not without saying that sometimes you'll feel that every step was followed beautifully and that it still didn't work out. Sometimes this will be the case, but in the market, your goal is to pick more winners than losers, or to have your good holdings outperform your not so good ones.

While I cannot promise that you'll never pick a bad stock again, I can say that with this formula, I have found consistent success; ranking in the top 3% of all analysts, columnists, hedge funds, and retail investors on the Motley Fool CAPs rating system. In other words, you may not find perfection, but your bad investments will be fewer and further between, and you'll remove much of the complexity and confusion while proceeding to invest in solid top-performing stocks.

References

(n.d.). Retrieved from Apple.com:
   http://investor.apple.com/secfiling.cfm?filingid=119312
   5-11-282113&cik=

(n.d.). Retrieved from riteaid.com:
   https://www.riteaid.com/corporate/investor-
   relations/quarterly-
   results?p_p_id=riteaidpressreleases_WAR_riteaidpressr
   eleasesportlet&p_p_lifecycle=0&p_p_state=normal&p_
   p_mode=view&p_p_col_id=column-
   3&p_p_col_count=1&_riteaidpressreleases_WAR_riteai
   dpressrel

(2013, November 7). Retrieved from 9to5mac.com:
   http://9to5mac.com/2013/11/07/apples-sapphire-deal-
   to-increase-manufacturers-revenue-from-sapphire-by-
   appr

(2014, June). Retrieved from edgaronline.com:
   http://yahoo.brand.edgar-
   online.com/displayfilinginfo.aspx?FilingID=10120552-
   1011-229428&type=sect&TabIn

*Apple to build new manufacturing facility in Arizona with solar-
   power, will create 2000+ jobs.* (2013, November 4).
   Retrieved from 9to5mac.com:
   http://9to5mac.com/2013/11/04/apple-to-build-
   manufacturing-facility-in-mesa-arizona-will-create-
   2000-jobs/

Home Depot. (2013, June 25). Retrieved from
   ir.homedepot.com:

http://ir.homedepot.com/phoenix.zhtml?p=irol-eventDetails&c=63646&eventID=5163205

Jacobs to Become Chairman and Chief Executive Officer. (2011, June 14). Retrieved from businesswire.com: http://www.businesswire.com/news/home/201106140 06005/en/Bradley-S.-Jacobs-Lead-Equity-Investment-150#.U-6-K_ldVzB

McCracken, J. (2014, July 30). *XPO Pulls Off 50 Purchases While Bypassing Wall Street.* Retrieved from Bloomberg: http://www.bloomberg.com/news/2014-07-29/xpo-s-jacobs-pulls-off-500-deals-bypassing-wall-street-bankers.html?cmpid=yhoo

Nichols, B. (2014, May 9). *Bradley Jacobs Interview.* Retrieved from Motley Fool: http://www.fool.com/investing/general/2014/05/09/br adley-jacobs-interview-4-key-takeaways-from-xp-2.aspx

Seeking Alpha. (2014, June 11). *Q1 2014 Earnings Call Transcript*. Retrieved from http://seekingalpha.com/article/2264763-restoration-hardware-holdings-rh-ceo-gary-friedman-on-q1-2014-results-earnings-call-transcript

Stone, K. (n.d.). Retrieved from pharma.about.com: http://pharma.about.com/od/BigPharma/a/Which-Popular-Drugs-Are-Going-Off-Patent-In-2013-2016.htm

U.S. Census Bureau News. (2014, August 13). Retrieved from census.gov: http://www.census.gov/retail/marts/www/marts_curre nt.pdf